Day of + Redemption

A Tenebrae Service and
Worship Drama for
Good Friday

Douglas W. Orbaker and Robert A. Blake

C.S.S. Publishing Co., Inc.

Lima, Ohio

DAY OF REDEMPTION

7807 / ISBN 0-89536-848-X   PRINTED IN U.S.A.

Table of Contents

Part 1

Part 2

Part 1

Seven Words to Us

A Tenebrae Service

Notes on the Service

This service includes a separate section for each of the Seven Last Words From The Cross. Each section contains a brief reading from the Passion narrative, and some kind of a litany, dramatic reading, or dialogue. In the case of the reading on "My God, My God, Why Have You Forsaken Me?" the additional reading is another Scripture passage, Psalm 22.

Each section gives way to the next with music and the extinguishing of a set of lights. We have not included the pieces of music which we used, because it is probably helpful to have music which is familiar to your congregation, at least for the hymns. Special music also depends largely on the musical tastes and abilities of your congregation.

We used several readers or leaders for each section of the service. In this way we involved many lay people as well as the pastors of the participating churches. Enough people will be needed to fill the following roles described in the service:

Leader of Call To Worship
Scripture Reader
Prayer of Confession and Litany of Forgiveness
Angry Thief
Repentant Thief
Male Leader for Litany on Mother and Brothers
Female Leader for Litany on Mother and Brothers
Four Readers for Dramatic Reading
Defeated Disciple
Victorious Disciple
Two Leaders for the Litany of Commitment

Except for the Scripture Reader and Leader of Call To Worship, everyone else may be seated in the worship area. This preserves for the service the feeling that this worship is arising from within the People of God. In order to do this, people will need to practice in order to speak loudly and clearly enough to be heard.

When the last of the lights have been extinguished, wait at least a minute in complete silence. Then from somewhere in the sanctuary a single voice begins to sing "Were You There?" The others who have taken part in the service should be prepared to join the singing on the second verse. Hearing this, most of the congregation will join in.

We encouraged people to leave in silence. We discovered later that several families remained in silence all the way home. This can become a moving and dramatic service of worship.

— Douglas Orbaker

A Good Friday Tenebrae Service
Based on the Seven Words From The Cross

Call to Worship (Lamentations 1:12 and Isaiah 53:5)

Leader: Does this mean nothing to you, all you who pass by?
People: Look, see if there is any sorrow like my sorrow.
Leader: He was wounded for our transgressions, he was bruised for our iniquities.
People: Upon him was the chastisement that made us whole, and with his stripes we are healed.

Hymn

Part 1

Scripture: Luke 23:32-38

Prayer of Confession: Everlasting and Merciful God, you are always more ready to forgive than we are to repent. We remember this day the suffering and death of our Lord Jesus Christ, and confess to you our shame in the sins which crucified him. Grant us grace that we may be reconciled to you, through your Son and our Lord. Amen

A Litany on Forgiveness

Leader: When They came to the place called "the skull" they crucified Jesus there, and Jesus said:
People: Father forgive them! For they don't know what they are doing.
Leader: For denying Jesus;
People: Father, forgive them, forgive us.
Leader: For running away at the time of need;
People: Father, forgive them, forgive us.
Leader: For mockings, beatings and insults;
People: Father, forgive them, forgive us.
Leader: For just following orders that bring about crucifixion;
People: Father, forgive them, forgive us.

Leader: For the cross on which Jesus died, and for the crosses
we erect on which we hang our sisters and brothers;
People: Father, forgive us! For we don't know what we are
doing.

Special Music
(Extinguish first set of lights)

Part 2

Scripture: Luke 23:39-43

Drama for Good Friday — "The Escape" (Optional)

Dialogue of Two Thieves
Angry Thief: We've struggled so hard. Why don't you help? Save
yourself and us!
Repentent Thief: My evil struggling is over. Jesus, remember me.
Angry Thief: The Romans are the ones who are evil. Their evil
justifies whatever we've done. Save yourself and us!
Repentent Thief: The evil of the Romans doesn't excuse my evil
in stealing from them. Jesus, remember me.
Angry Thief: And you claim to be the Messiah. This is some way
to lead Israel. Save yourself and us!
Repentent Thief: Maybe your kingdom really is different. Jesus,
Remember me.
Angry Thief: We trusted in you! You're dashing our hopes,
destroying our dreams. Save yourself and us!
Repentent Thief: I may deserve this, you don't. Jesus, remember
me.
Hymn
(Extinguish Second set of lights)

Part 3

Scripture: John 19:25-27

A Litany on Jesus' Mother and Brothers
(Based on Matthew 12:46-50)

Leader: To create a family, with new sons and daughters,
(Woman) new mothers and fathers, all sisters and brothers.

10

People:	"Woman, Here is your son. Here is your mother."
Leader: *(Man)*	Jesus was still talking to people when his mother and brothers arrived. They stood outside asking to speak with him.
People:	"Woman, Here is your son. Here is your mother."
Leader: *(Woman)*	So one of the people there said to him, "Look, your mother and brothers are standing outside, and they want to speak with you."
People:	"Woman, Here is your son. Here is your mother."
Leader: *(Man)*	Jesus answered, "Who is my mother? Who are my brothers?"
People:	"Woman, Here is your son. Here is your mother."
Leader: *(Woman)*	Then he pointed to his disciples and said, "Look! Here are my mother and my brothers!"
People:	"Woman, Here is your son. Here is your mother."
Leader: *(Man)*	For the person who does what my Father in Heaven wants is my brother, my sister, my mother."
People:	"Woman, Here is your son. Here is your mother."
Leader: *(Woman)*	To create a family, with new sons and daughters, new mothers and fathers, all sisters and brothers.
People:	May we behold each other: brother, sister, mother and father with that love. Amen

Hymn
(Extinguish Third set of lights)

Part 4

Scriptures: Mark 15:33-39, Psalm 22: 1-11 and 19-31

Special Music
(Extinguish Fourth set of lights)

Part 5

Scripture: John 19:28-29

Dramatic Reading
Reader 1: He was thirsty for God.

Reader 2: He was thirsty for human souls.

Reader 3: He was thirsty for the acceptance of others.

Reader 4: No, the sun was hot, he was in pain, he was dying. He was thirsty.

Reader 1: Did the soldiers offer wine to mock him?

Reader 2: Did the soldiers offer wine to drug him?

Reader 3: Did the soldiers offer wine as an act of compassion?

Reader 4: Did the soldiers offer wine just to make him be quiet?

Reader 1: Jesus was God, above the physical hurts of the body.

Leader 2: Jesus was God's Son. His relationship with the Father didn't let physical pain interfere.

Reader 3: Yes, But Jesus was also man. His lips were dry, His throat was parched. He was thirsty.

Reader 4: The divinity of Jesus thirsts for our committed love.

Reader 1: The humanity of Jesus thirsts for relationships with people who understand.

Reader 2: And the body of Jesus is thirsty.

Reader 3: May we lift our committed love and our understanding relationships to him.

Reader 4: And may we quench the thirst of his people in his name.

Hymn
(Extinguish Fifth set of lights)

Part 6

Scripture: John 19:30

Dialogue on "It Is Finished"
Defeated: (sadly) It is finished, He is going to die.

Victorious: (joyously) It is finished. The terrible task is completed.

Defeated: It is finished. Our hopes and dreams are empty.

Victorious: It is finished. The world doesn't know it yet, but victory is assured.

Defeated: It is finished. Death and evil have won once again.

Victorious: It is finished. Death and evil will never again have the victory.

Defeated: It is finished. We might as well go back to our old lives, our old ways.

Victorious: It is finished. The old life is gone, the new life is coming.

Defeated: It is finished. We had thought he was the one to save Israel, but he is gone.

Victorious: It is finished. The triumph is at hand.

Special Music
(Extinguish Sixth set of lights)

Part 7

Scripture: Luke 23:44-49

A Litany of Commitment
Leader 1: The sun stopped shining and darkness covered the Earth for three hours.
People: Father, in your hand I place my spirit.
Leader 1: The curtain in the temple was torn in two.
People: Father, in your hand I place my spirit.
Leader 1: Even the centurian recognized Jesus' greatness.
People: Father, in your hand I place my spirit.
Leader 1: Even as darkness haunts our souls,
People: Even as our secret places are torn in two.
Leader 1: Even as others recognize the good we fail to see.
People: Father, in your hand we place our spirits.
Leader 2: When we forgive those who hurt us, or others forgive us,
People: When we ask for, and receive, your promise of salvation,
Leader 2: When we are concerned for those we love.
People: Father, in your hand we place our spirits.
Leader 2: When we feel all alone, and think that even you have abandoned us,
People: When the suffering of our bodies overwhelms our souls,
Leader 2: When things are so confusing we can't tell defeat from triumph.

People: Father, in your hand we place our spirits.
Leader 2: Even as death overtakes us,
People: Father, in your hand we place our spirits. Amen

(Extinguish Last set of lights)

Hymn: "Were You There?"

Following the final hymn, the congregation will leave in silence.

Part 2

The Escape

A Worship Drama

Notes on the Drama "The Escape"

Theudas and Barabbas are two Bible characters. About them we know little more than their names.

Theudas was a Jewish revolutionary who led about 400 men in an attempt to overthrow the Roman government. We read his name once — in the Book of Acts. The Pharisees who invoke Theudas' name in that context dismiss him in almost the same breath by saying:

. . he was slain and all who followed him were dispersed and came to nothing. (Acts 5:36)

We *do* know a little more about Barabbas. His name is mentioned near the end of all four Gospels, during the time of Jesus' trial.

We know Barabbas was the Roman prisoner the people wanted released, as was Pilate's custom during the Jewish Passover. Matthew 27:16 calls him a "notorious prisoner."

Mark 15:7 describes Barabbas as:

. . . among the rebels in prison, who had committed murder in the insurrection.

We know nothing else about that insurrection, except for Luke's comment in 23:19 that it first broke out in the city of Jerusalem. John 18:40 merely states that Barabbas was "a robber."

From what little evidence may be found in the biblical accounts, we could never be certain whether Barabbas and Theudas ever *knew* each other personally. We know only that they were both leaders in similar, unsuccessful attempts to overthrow the Roman government in Judea.

But suppose Theudas and Barabbas *did* know each other? Suppose they shared a cell together in the same prison at Jerusalem? Suppose, in fact, they found themselves both a part of the same events which surrounded Jesus' trial and crucifixion.

Perhaps this is what may have transpired . . .

The story takes place in a Roman prison in Jerusalem during the Jewish Passover festival. The time is early in the first century, around 33 AD. As the play opens, a small cell appears with a barred window to the center rear, and containing two cots, one on either side. There is a prisoner on each cot, staring at the ceiling.

(As the lights go on, the roar of a crowd is heard off-stage.)

Theudas

(He gets up from cot and goes to the window.) **Well, I see the natives are restless. I wonder what all the commotion is about out there.** *(He looks at Barabbas, as if trying to make conversation.)*

(*Barabbas lies motionless, as if not hearing him.*)

Theudas
(*He looks back out the window.*) The fickle crowd is probably framing another poor beggar. As if our blood won't be enough entertainment for them today. Or maybe it's just the excitement of the Passover festival. That is the celebration that's supposed to be going on now, isn't it? (*He looks to Barabbas.*)

(*Barabbas continues to ignore him.*)

Theudas
(*Irritated*) What's the matter with you? You suddenly go deaf over night? (*He rushes toward him, as if to grab him.*) Why don't you answer me?!

Barabbas
Touch me, and it won't be the smartest thing you ever did.

Theudas
(*He stops. Stalking over to his cot and sitting down, he attempts to smooth out the confrontation.*) Just trying to make conversation. It seems that while I talk, my words drown out my thoughts . . . my thoughts of . . . of what they're going to do to me — er, to us — today. Unless my friends can . . . (*He stops.*) Never mind. What are you thinking about?

Barabbas
(*He stares at him for a moment, as if trying to decide whether to speak. The he stares back at the ceiling.*) I'm thinking about a small house near Jericho . . . and a few sheep . . . and my father driving them toward our house. (*Pause.*) And I'm thinking about the cursed Roman soldiers who destroyed that house. And those sheep. And my father! And I'm thinking about some four hundred "friends" who swore they'd fight to the death to destroy the men who did it and throw off the yoke of this blasted government. But it didn't work out that way . . . Now, they're out there groveling in the dirt for Caesar, and I'm in here, talking to a senseless moron, and waiting for death!

Theudas

(After a few moments of uncomfortable silence) Well, I'm thinking about . . .

Barabbas

(Interrupting) I didn't ask!

Theudas

I know, but hear me out.

Barabbas

(He jumps up and begins to pace about.) Hear you out!? I've been hearing you all morning, and you make as much sense as that . . . that screaming mob out there.

Theudas

Listen, Barabbas. I've got some friends on the outside . . .

Barabbas

(Interrupting) Yeah! So do I! And they're probably out in that crowd whooping it up while I'm in this cell rotting. And they'll probably be out there tomorrow partying with your "friends" while the vultures are picking over my flesh . . . And yours, ol' buddy. So you might as well get used to . . .

Theudas

(Interrupting, at the point of hysteria) No! No! *(More composed)* I mean, no. Not my friends. Listen. My friends and I made a pact that if any one of us were captured, the rest would fight to the death to free him. And they will. You'll see.

Barabbas

And just where have these friends of yours been these past six months while you've been rotting here? Face the facts, man. They are at the same place that *my* friends are: out there, living, working, having babies, and totally oblivious to you and your plan. Face up to it. The only one concerned about you is *you.* *(Menacingly)* And tomorrow at this time you won't even have *that* consideration.

Theudas

No, they'll come. You'll see. They've just been waiting for the right moment. *(Trying to convince himself)* These things take careful planning. I'm sure they're waiting for the confusion of the festival to spring me.

Barabbas

Just like they used the confusion of the Tabernacle festival and the confusion of the Purim festival to spring you? Face it! Your friends have long since forgotten you. You're finished. Alone! Tomorrow at this time you'll be little more than a pile of rotting flesh, feeding the vultures and smelling up the countryside, just like me. *(He sits down on his cot.)*

Theudas

No! That's not true. I'm not like you! I'm an innocent man. God wouldn't let that happen to an innocent man.

Barabbas

Innocent!? Ha! You're a murderer, just like me! And everyone knows it.

Theudas

Yes, but I murdered for the sake of Jehovah, and for our nation. God will rescue me for that.

Barabbas

God — if there is one — is out there with your other friends who are supposedly going to rescue you. And he's probably just about as concerned for you as they are!

Theudas

No. He will reward me for my service to him.

Barabbas

Your service to *him!?* Who are you kidding? You haven't done anything for anybody but yourself. Your "service" was your plan to be the big shot who led a successful rebellion against Rome. You had big plans of how you'd be the head honcho, maybe even the Messiah, with everyone bowing down to you and singing your praises. And when your empire of 400 men comes crumbling down around your ear, you cry out to God to save you for your "service" to him. Your service . . .! You're nothing more than a fraud and a hypocrite!

Theudas
Why don't you go to Hell!

Barabbas
I will! And while I'm stoking the fires on number 8, you'll be stoking the fires on number 9, right along there with me.

Theudas
Where do you get off judging me? *(Sarcastically)* I'm sure you're an innocent victim of society.

Barabbas
No. I'm guilty. I killed two hundred of those Roman swine, and given the opportunity, I'd kill two hundred more. But I'm not sitting around whining what a great mother's son I am, and hoping for some worthless friend — or non-existent God — to rescue me.

Theudas
Then what are you hoping for?

Barabbas
The same thing that you'd be hoping for, if you had any sense: an executioner with an excellent aim and a sharp sword. A miserable existence that ends in a blanket of night, not in agony as you quiver in the dust of his first blow, begging him to finish his task, so the pain will cease! That's the only thing to hope for. *(Flops down prostrate on his cot.)*

(A Roman guard enters.)

Guard
All right, scum. On your feet.

Barabbas
You're already on your feet!

Guard

(He stiffens in rage, then relaxes. He speaks with contempt.)
Very funny. We'll see if your sense of humor is up to par later
on today when the executioner tickles your throat. The
Procurator, Pilate, sent me here to choose which of you dogs
he should consider for pardon. With that remark, you may
have just simplified my task.

Barabbas

(Sarcastically) You mean our old buddy Pilate is going soft
in his old age? What would our hero Caesar have to say?

Guard

No, he's not going soft. It has something to do with a loop-
hole in the Roman law that allows him to put one of you
dogs back onto the streets every year. As if there wasn't
enough trash out there already.

Theudas

(Taking hope) Yeah! I've heard of that custom. Every year
during the Passover festival, the Procurator is permitted to
release a prisoner. But Pilate hasn't done that for years. Why
is he doing it now?

Guard

How should I know? If I had my way, I'd kill all of you and
empty this cesspool of all its garbage. But, I have my
orders. *(Teasingly)* Of course, if you — uh — gentlemen would
prefer I not enter your name in the competition, I'll just . . .

Theudas

(Interrupting) No! Wait!

Guard

(Looks to Theudas) What's your name?

Theudas

(Expectantly) Theudas, sir.

Guard

What's your crime?

Theudas

A mistake, sir.

Guard

A mistake?

Theudas

Yes, a mistake. You see, I happened to be among a crowd of people near a murdered Roman soldier. Poor fellow. Just doing his duty when . . . Well, anyway, being a victim of circumstances, I was convicted of the crime and sentenced to die. But I'm innocent. You see, I love the Roman government, and if released, I'm sure I could be of benefit to it. My people, the Jews, they loved and respected me before this awful experience, and if relesed, I could surely influence them for Caesar. I would be eternally grateful to you if you can have me released. My family does have some money which . . . if you could . . .

Guard

(Interrupting) I don't make the decisions. Pilate does. I merely give him the names of the prisoners being held, and their crimes. (He thinks for a moment, then speaks, greedily.) But I may be able to present a favorable picture to Pilate of a Jew beloved of his countrymen, and who loves the Roman government, and who . . . uh . . . always pays his debts?

Theudas

Yes!! Yes!!

Guard

(Looking to Barabbas) What's your name?

Barabbas

Barabbas!

Guard

And your crime?

Barabbas

(Mockingly) A mistake, sir!

Guard
(Glancing at Theudas) Seems to be a lot . . . What's *your* mistake?

Barabbas
(He thinks a moment.) Actually, two mistakes.

Guard
Two!?

Barabbas
Yeah, two. One is that I got caught.

Barabbas
(With growing irritation) And the other . . .

Barabbas
The other is that I only killed 200 of you pigs instead of 2,000 before I got caught!

Guard
(He stiffens in rage.) Why, you . . .! (More composed and calculating) You just signed your death certificate with that crack, wise guy. (As if formulating a report in his mind) Let's see. Prisoner's name: Barabbas. Prisoner's crime: murdering 200 Roman soldiers. Despised and hated by the Jews and a threat to the Roman government. That report ought to rid us of you, permanently! I'll be back for you as soon as I make my report and Pilate decides. You're a dead man! (Stalks out.)

Barabbas
(Shouting after him) That'll probably be the first honest report you've ever made!

Theudas
(To Barabbas) You see! You see! I told you Jehovah would get me out of here. I told you.

Barabbas
That's odd. I distinctly remember you telling me that it would be your *friends* that would get you out of here.

Theudas

(With piety) Jehovah could have used my friends. But Jehovah sometimes chooses to work in strange ways.

Barabbas

He must. He's arranging the release of a coward and a fake for his service. You make me sick! *(Mocking previous scene)* Yes, sir. I'm innocent, sir. I'll be eternally grateful, sir . . . Well, you're not free yet.

Theudas

I had to lie, Barabbas. I just had to. The thought of my life ending — of not existing — and the awful pain of death . . . *(In agony)* I just couldn't stand it.

Barabbas

Then we have something in common — I can't stand you!

Theudas

(Trying to justify himself) I suppose you don't want to live!

Barabbas

What is there to live for? An insurrection that has no hope of succeeding? A God who is unable to rescue you without your help? Friends or family that have long since deserted you? What is there to live for?

Theudas

There must be something . . .

Barabbas

(Interrupting) Yeah! There's something to live for. Yourself! That's right. Old number one — me!

Theudas

Isn't that enough?

Barabbas

No! Not for me. It ceased to be a long time ago. I'm sick of myself, of who I am, of my very existence! And if you weren't such a coward, you'd admit the same thing.

(The guard enters.)

Guard

Pilate has decided. You're free to go. *(Theudas jumps up joyfully. Guard stops him.)* Not you. Barabbas!

Barabbas

(Incredulously) Me!? Why me?

Guard

Pilate makes the decisions, not me. His orders are to release you and *(Motions off stage)* put this man in your place.

Barabbas

Who is he? What has he done?

Guard

(Sarcastically) Oh, the prisoner has now become a judge. Maybe you'd have me convince Pilate to change his mind. *(Pointing off stage)* Go!!

(Barabbas leaves haltingly, as if he still can't believe it's all happening.)

Theudas

But . . . But, what about me?

Guard

(Sarcastically) You? You will have the privilege of being crucified with the KING OF THE JEWS! *(The lights go out.)*

About the Authors

Douglas Orbaker is pastor of Cranston Memorial Presbyterian Church, New Richmond, Ohio. He is a graduate of Grove City (Pennsylvania) College; Louisville (Kentucky) Presbyterian Seminary; and McCormick Theological Seminary, Chicago, Illinois. He previously served Condit Presbyterian Church, Sunbury, Ohio.

Robert A. Blake is pastor of Spiceland (Indiana) Friends Meeting. He is a graduate of Loop Junior College and Moody Bible Institute, both in Chicago; Trinity College, Deerfield, Illinois; and Earlham School of Religion, Richmond, Indiana. Prior to his present position Pastor Blake served Arba (Indiana) Friends Meeting.